Schirmer's Library of Musical Classics

Vol. 782

CHARLES DE BÉRIOT
Op. 104

CONCERTO No. IX
IN A MINOR
FOR
VIOLIN

WITH ACCOMPANIMENT OF
ORCHESTRA

EDITED AND FINGERED
BY
HENRY SCHRADIECK

G. SCHIRMER, Inc.

DISTRIBUTED BY

HAL•LEONARD®
CORPORATION
7777 W BLUEMOUND RD PO BOX 13819 MILWAUKEE, WI 53213

Concerto IX.

CH. de BERIOT. Op. **104.**

Schirmer's Library of Musical Classics

Vol. 782

CHARLES DE BÉRIOT
OP. 104

CONCERTO No. IX
IN A MINOR
FOR
VIOLIN

WITH ACCOMPANIMENT OF
ORCHESTRA

EDITED AND FINGERED
BY
HENRY SCHRADIECK

VIOLIN

G. SCHIRMER, Inc.

DISTRIBUTED BY

HAL•LEONARD®
CORPORATION
7777 W BLUEMOUND RD PO BOX 13819 MILWAUKEE, WI 53213

Concerto IX.

Violin.

Allegro maestoso.
Tutti

CH. de BÉRIOT. Op. 104.

Violin.

Violin.

Violin.

Rondo.
Allegretto moderato.

Violin.

Violin.

Rondo.
Allegretto moderato.